YOUR BEST LIFE S

How to Uncover Your
COMPELLING CORE VALUES
The Foundation for Living Your Best Life

MICHAEL E. ANGIER

Published by Success Networks International, Inc.
Tampa Bay, Florida 34609-9509

www.SuccessNet.org

ISBN: 9781698327983

Limit of Liability/Disclaimer of Warranty

The Top 10 Reasons to Know and Live Your Core Values

1. Gain Real Clarity about who you are and what you stand for. To get what you truly want, you must *be* who you truly are.

2. Better Use of Time. You make better choices about where you spend your time—your most valuable asset. There's no way to get any more of it. To live an ideal life, you must learn to choose carefully as to how you invest your time and energy. Your core values should be your guide.

3. More Income. Being true to your core values affects your bottom line. It's a lot easier to earn money when you're doing what you love in accordance with your core values.

4. Purpose and Passion. Knowing and being true to what really matters to you means having more passion in your purpose and more purpose in your passion. The congruity makes it happen.

5. Inspiration. Understanding and living from your core values opens the door to more inspiration in your life. And we can all use more of that.

6. Motivation. Living in accordance with your core values keeps you motivated. It's motivation from within rather than motivation plastered on from the outside.

7. Overcome Discouragement. We all experience challenges and we all get discouraged from time to time. But when you know what your most important values are and are dedicated to making them live and breathe in your life, you become more resilient.

8. Stay On Track. Your values are like your moral compass. They keep you headed toward your true north. And when you get off course, you notice sooner. They help you get back on track more easily.

9. Easier Choice of Goals. Choosing which goals you set and go after is easier when you're clear on your most important values. You can do anything you want, but you can't do *everything*. It's incumbent upon you to choose wisely. And that's easier when your values are front and center all the time.

10. Better Decisions. Being clear on your core values helps every decision easier to make. Weighing the pros and cons of any decision is simply less painful and less complicated.

In short, discovering, defining and living your core values allows you to get more of the right things done and enjoy the journey more.

Table of Contents

Introduction

I commend you for taking upon yourself the worthy endeavor of getting clear on and living in congruence with your core values.

You can now begin to reap the many rewards of having the passion, power, meaning and significance that comes from building upon a solid foundation of core values.

Objectives

The intention of this book is to help you understand the value and importance of knowing your core values and living your life in accordance with them.

The knowledge and understanding you gain from this process will create a solid foundation for designing, creating and living your best life.

Designed with You in Mind

This process is for those individuals who are not—and cannot—be satisfied with mediocrity. It's for people who care about things that matter—who want to make a difference.

It's for those who want to live their best life.

If you want to be inspired instead of just motivated, if you want to be driven from within and feel a passion for your work and your life, then *Your Compelling Core Values* is for you.

This book is NOT for you . . . .

If you're looking for the quick fix or the flash-in-the-pan success.

But if you want success in many things—the kind of success that lasts, the kind of success that can give you inner peace—this *is* for you.

In this Book You'll Discover

- how to get clear on and articulate your core values

- how your core values drive your purpose

- how to have more passion in your purpose and purpose in your passion

- how to stay inspired and face down discouragement

- how to prioritize your goals and tasks to get more of the right things done

- how to notice if, when, and why you're off-course

- how to stay focused on what matters most

Each Chapter Builds Upon the Last

- You're given access to valuable resources.

- You begin to live your purpose grounded in the bedrock of your core values.

- Who you truly are begins to really shine forth.

Live Your Purpose

Not only will you be more successful, you will enjoy your success more. You'll also achieve your purpose with less effort and conflict.

What you discover can be implemented not only in your own life but also in your family. It can also be employed in a business or any organization. It works in all of them.

Creating Excellence

In order to create excellence there must be a strong foundation to build upon. Build that foundation with solid values and a strong sense of purpose, and the results are nothing short of miraculous.

It matters not whether you make widgets, serve clients or sell other people's products. You can do it with purpose, passion and meaning.

You can create excellence, provide fulfillment and create substantial profits at the same time.

Self Actualization

This is how Abraham Mazlow described self-actualization. He said that it was a "bringing together of what I do and what I really value." And that's exactly what this book is about.

I'm confident you'll enjoy and benefit from participating in the fulfilling process of discovering your core values and orienting your life around them—as so many others have.

Set Yourself Up to Win

Be sure to schedule time to study and act upon the information you're being given. Do that now and make a commitment to finishing this book and this process.

Assignment/Action Step

Reflect on what kind of decisions you have made in the last few days.

Why are you choosing to do—or *not* do—certain things?

What values might you be honoring or not honoring?

This is not a time to make yourself wrong for any decisions you have made. This is a time to just notice and be aware.

Chapter 1:
Your Best Life Defined

"Decide what kind of life you really want . . . And then, say no to everything that isn't that."

Are You Seeking Your Best Life?

Before we get into the nitty gritty of discovering, articulating and living your core values, let's take a look at some objectives.

If you're reading this, I assume you want a better life. You want to improve on where you are. Maybe a little. Maybe a lot.

Regardless of where you find yourself at this point in time—and regardless of your age—you can certainly improve. After all, the biggest room in the world is the room for improvement.

You may be wanting to take your already on-purpose, values-driven, comfortable life and simply make it better.

Or maybe your life is a train wreck.

Either way, you have to start with the end in mind.

It's important to acknowledge where you are, but there will be plenty of time for that. What's more important is getting clear on where you're going.

Your best life doesn't just happen. It doesn't automatically unfold, and it's certainly not handed to you. You have to design and create your best life yourself. Because if you don't, other people and outside circumstances will do it for you. And do you know what other people and outside circumstances have planned for you? Hardly anything at all.

"You have to design and create your best life yourself. Because if you don't, other people and outside circumstances will do it for you. And do you know what other people and outside circumstances have planned for you? Hardly anything at all."

What Does Your Best Life Look Like?

No doubt you have some idea about what your Best Life looks like. I assume you have some goals—some things you want to accomplish or experience before you make your departure from planet Earth.

Have you ever envisioned, in great detail, how you would like to have your life unfold? Do you see it? Can you taste it? Do you believe it? Can you imagine how it feels?

The clearer you can become on all the things you want in your life—and the reasons why—the easier it will be to do what you need to do to achieve them.

We all want to be happy, and I personally believe we are happiest when we are in pursuit of our highest and best.

For now, let me share with you, in general terms, what I mean by your Best Life. It should give you some seminal ideas for your Best Life Plan.

It's a tall order, but I think your Best Life is a life without regrets.

---

*"Your Best Life is a life
without regrets."*

Your Best Life is a life by design—not default.

I think you should build a life from which you don't need a vacation. Not that you won't *take* vacations, but you won't *need* them. Because your vocation will be your avocation. And it's not a struggle; it's a wiggle.

Your Best Life requires your best self. If you want your life to get better, *you* have to get better. I'm guessing that's why you're reading this book.

> *"Your Best Life requires*
> *your best self."*

For me it means rising to a calling instead of an alarm clock. I get up when I *want* to get up, and I use an alarm clock only once or twice a year. It is possible.

I believe your Best Life is a life of clarity, purpose, passion and prosperity. A life designed around your values, principles and intentions.

Simply put—a life on your terms. You get to design, define, create and live Your Best Life.

Top Seven Results of Living Your Best Life

The following seven benefits are what I consider the biggest payoffs for creating a life well lived.

1. Significance & Meaning

2. Time, Location & Financial Freedom

3. Happiness, Fun & Adventure

4. Purpose & Integrity

5. Confidence & Self-esteem

6. Rich Relationships

7. Health, Fitness & Vitality

Sounds worthwhile, yes?

Your full and unique potential is unknown. But certainly worth going for, don't you think? Who can count the number of apples that can come from a single apple seed?

The Path to Your Best Life

The illustration below shows what I see as the best path to your best life—however you might define it. The bottom four tiers are foundational. The top three are much more dynamic. But they should stand in the service of your core values, purpose, mission and vision.

The Path to Your Best Life

Anything, Not Everything

My belief is that you can do *anything* in this life. But you can't do *everything*. That's why it's so important to choose your goals, your projects and your tasks wisely. And to base them on the foundational steps of your core values, purpose, mission and vision.

> *"You can do* anything *you want in this life. You just can't do* everything *you want."*

Otherwise, you're making choices and spending your precious time and energy on your own or others' whims.

Getting clear on your core values, your purpose and your mission will help you to avoid regrets and feel like you invested your life in the best way possible. From that you can create a Vivid Vision for this great life of yours.

> *"Life should not be a journey to the grave with the intention of arriving safely in a pretty and well-preserved body, but rather to skid in broadside in a cloud of smoke, thoroughly used up, totally worn out, and loudly proclaiming 'Wow, what a ride!'"*
>
> —Hunter S. Thompson

The bottom line is that unless you invest the time, energy and money in creating a life you truly want, you're going to be spending a lot of time and effort supporting a life you *don't* want.

> *"Unless you invest the time, energy and money in creating a life you truly want, you're going to be spending a lot of time and effort supporting a life you don't want."*

Action Steps

This book is based on our most popular course. And if you learn better in a more structured *course* environment, you may want to consider this engaging and dynamic home-study video course on discovering and clarifying your core values. To find out more, go to www.YourCoreValues.com

It's nominally priced. Thousands of people have taken this course and are living more purpose-driven lives because of the process.

"Life should not be a journey to the grave with the intention of arriving safely in a pretty and well-preserved body, but rather to skid in broadside in a cloud of smoke, thoroughly used up, totally worn out, and loudly proclaiming 'Wow, what a ride!' "

—Hunter S. Thompson

The bottom line is that unless you invest the time, energy and money in creating a life you truly want, you're going to be spending a lot of time and effort supporting a life you *don't* want.

"Unless you invest the time, energy and money in creating a life you truly want, you're going to be spending a lot of time and effort supporting a life you don't want."

Action Steps

Please consider this engaging and inspiring home-study video course on discovering and clarifying your core values. To find out more, go to www.YourCoreValues.com

It's nominally priced. Thousands of people have taken this course and are living more purpose-driven lives because of the process.

Chapter 2:
Building on Firm Foundations

In this chapter we start to lay the groundwork for the rest of the process.

We begin some discussions that illuminate what's truly important to you. And in doing so, you start to live your life in harmony with the values you already have.

Living the Good Life

We all want to be successful. And that's different for everyone.

The good news is that we live in a day and age that allows us to design our own lives—to decide what's really important to us.

Our success is how we define it.

Know This

Something to be aware of . . . The 'why-to' of this process is more important than the 'how-to'.

I ask you to trust the process. This is not complicated, but it is valuable.

OK, let's get going.

Discovery

Developing your core values does not mean *inventing* them.

It means uncovering and discovering what they already are.

Before digital photography, our cameras took pictures with film and they needed to be developed. And like developing a photograph in a darkroom, we bring forth what is already imprinted upon the paper but is perhaps not yet clear.

Only Some Succeed

Why do some people succeed and others fail? That's one of the key questions I've been asking myself and others for over 40 years.

I've found many reasons for failure, but the most common is a lack of consistency in striving for and achieving goals.

Most People Just Don't Stick it Out

Anyone can do what's required to achieve their goals for a day or even a week.

But it's a rare person who continues on in their quest and is able to endure the hardship and sacrifices with which we are inevitably faced.

Determination

So how do you stay true to your purpose? How do you maintain your belief? How do you avoid the temptation of taking shortcuts?

We all need support. You may need systems or people or programs to provide that support and help you keep on keeping on.

These are important and every single person I've ever encountered who was successful had some kind of support mechanism. They didn't do it alone.

It's Up to You

The support I found consistent with every person of achievement was the support of their values. They were true to their own values.

"Every person of achievement had the support of their values. They were true to their own values. All the great men and women of history were mostly congruent with who they were and what they stood for."

All the great men and women of history were mostly congruent with who they were and what they stood for.

You might not even agree with their values as being virtuous, but they were true to them nonetheless.

Build on Solid Foundation

It worked for them and it can work for you.

People who have it together are people who are clear on their values. They know who they are and what they stand for.

You can be one of those people.

The Values Model

If you'd like, you can download your own copy of the graphic below using this link.

www.SuccessNet.org/files/YCVModel.pdf

Print two or three copies for yourself to use as worksheets.

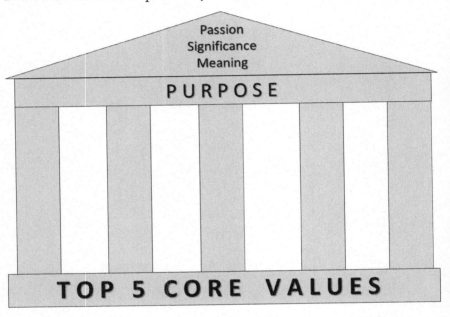

As you can see, this model resembles a temple—a building with pillars and a roof. *The pillars are your core values.*

They support your purpose and enable you to experience passion, meaning and significance in your life.

They give value to your efforts and enable you to experience true fulfillment.

Your Top 5 Core Values

In the next chapter, you'll begin the process of narrowing down your list of the many things you hold dear into **five key core values.**

When you determine your top five, you'll write them onto the pillars in the Values Model.

This Works for All

I've applied this model to people, companies, teams, marriages and associations. It can even be applied to countries. It works for all.

Consider it a clarity tool to help you not only visualize but also be reminded of what's really important and what you're building your life upon.

What are You Building?

I like the story of a man who was walking by a large construction site and paused to watch what was going on.

One of the workers was close to the fence and the man asked what he was doing. The worker appeared irritated and in a sarcastic tone said, "What do you think I'm doing? I'm laying bricks!"

The onlooker nodded and continued to watch. He then asked another worker what *he* was doing. This one was only slightly more pleasant. "I'm hauling bricks, can't you see?"

Michael E. Angier

The bystander continued watching but asked a third worker the same question. To this, the worker replied with a smile and said, "I'm building a cathedral!"

All of the workers were doing similar work, but one was doing it from an entirely different perspective. He was focusing on what he was accomplishing instead of what he was doing.

And that makes all the difference.

When you know what you're doing, why you're doing it, and it's consistent with your values, you experience things in a totally different way.

Action Steps

What's Important to You?

- Ask yourself and even others what they value most.

- Ask questions like:

    1. If you could have what you really wanted, what would it be?

    2. What's the most important thing in your life?

    3. What do you care about more than anything else?

    4. What is in your life that you *don't* want?

    5. Are you spending your time on what matters most?

"If you keep doing what you've always done, you'll end up with what you've always gotten."

Michael E. Angier

Chapter 3:
Creating Your Initial Values List

How Did it Go?

I trust you've done the assignment from the previous chapter.

Who did you talk to? Interesting, wasn't it?

I've come to learn that it's easy to listen to people when they're telling the truth—when they're talking about something that really matters to them.

"Clarity Leads to Power"

This statement is more profound than you might think at first glance.

Of all the people and companies I've coached and counseled, I've found that knowing what they wanted was often the hardest thing to elicit from them.

Once they got clear on what they wanted and the *reasons* why they wanted it, success was virtually assured.

It's the same with values.

If you know what they are and can articulate them, you can live them. But if they're ambiguous, your results will be ambiguous as well.

> *"If you know your top core values and can articulate them, you can live them. But if they're ambiguous, your results will be ambiguous as well. "*

Check Out Our Core Values List

The following list can also be found as a worksheet downloadable from our website. Simply go to www.Successnet.org/files/valueslist.pdf for your free copy.

Download the list and begin to sift it down to a more manageable number. Then, go through the list and circle any of the words that are particularly important to you.

Look for words that resonate with you—words that have some feeling attached to them.

No "Shoulding" on Yourself

This is not a time to 'should' on yourself. These are *your* values.

Don't pick out what you think they *should* be but rather what they actually are. But don't think *too* much. Your best choices will usually be your first inclinations.

I suggest doing this at least two different times with different colored pens. The reason being that your moods may affect your choices.

Abundance, prosperity	Acceptance
Accomplishment	Accountability
Accuracy	Achievement
Acknowledgement	Action
Adaptability	Adventure
Affection	Ambition
Appreciation	Attitude
Attractiveness	Authenticity
Awareness	Beauty, aesthetics
Being capable	Being different
Benevolence	Boldness
Bravery	Career
Caring	Challenge
Change	Children
Civility	Clarity
Class	Comfort
Commitment	Communication
Compassion	Community
Competency	Competition
Confidence	Confidentiality
Connection, collaboration	Consistency
Contribution, service	Cooperation
Courage	Courtesy

Creativity, creation	Credibility
Customer satisfaction	Decency
Dedication	Delight
Determination	Dignity
Directness	Discovery
Discipline	Diversity
Dreams	Duty
Education	Effectiveness
Efficiency	Elegance
Empathy	Empowerment
Enlightenment	Equality
Ethics	Excellence, mastery
Exploration, discovery	Expression
Fairness	Faith
Faithful	Fame
Family	Financial health, prosperity
Financial security	Fitness
Flexibility	Focus
Forgiveness	Freedom, liberty
Friendship	Fun, joy
Generosity	Grace
Growth	Hard work
Harmony	Health, wellness, fitness

Heart	Honesty, integrity
Honor	Hope
Hospitality	Humor
Imagination	Inclusion
Independence	Individuality
Industry	Influence
Innovation	Inquisitiveness
Insight	Inspiration
Integrity	Intelligence
Intimacy, romance	Intuition
Invention, innovation	Justice
Kindness	Knowledge
Leadership	Learning
Liberty	Longevity
Love	Loyalty
Making a difference	Mastery
Mentoring	Morality
Nature	Nurturing
Objectivity	Openness
Opportunity	Orderliness, organization
Passion	Patriotism
Peace	Perseverance
Planning	Playfulness

Pleasure	Positive attitude
Possibility	Power
Practicality	Prestige
Productivity	Professionalism
Profits, profitability	Prosperity, abundance
Protection	Prudence
Quality of life	Quest
Recognition	Reliability
Renewal	Research
Resilience	Respect
Responsibility	Results
Risk-taking	Safety
Security	Self-awareness
Self-control	Self-expression
Self-respect	Sensitivity
Serenity	Service
Sharing	Simplicity
Sincerity	Skills
Solidarity	Sophistication
Speed	Spirituality, religion
Spontaneity	Spouse
Stability	Stewardship
Strength	Support

Success, victory	Symbiosis
Synergy	Teaching
Teamwork	Temperance
Thinking	Thoughtfulness
Timeliness	Tolerance
Tradition	Trust, trustworthiness
Truth	Understanding
Vision	Vitality, zest
Wealth	Winning
Wisdom	

Action Step

In the next chapter, we talk about narrowing this list down. If you want to get a jumpstart, put a star next to those most important values you circled.

Do this for only about 12-20 items.

I know it's not easy to make these choices, but remember that you're not *discarding* the values you are not selecting—only focusing on those that are of the utmost importance—on what matters most.

Michael E. Angier

Chapter 4:
Finalizing Your Top 5 Core Values

---

*"A person who won't stand
for something will fall for
anything."*

—Zig Ziglar

Big Rocks First

I once heard a story about a college professor who wanted to drive home an important point to his students.

He announced it was time for a quiz. He placed a one-gallon, wide-mouthed Mason jar on the table in front of him and then inserted a dozen or more fist-sized rocks into the jar.

"Is the jar full," he asked. "Yes", they all replied.

"Really"?

He reached under the table and brought out a bucket of gravel and poured it in as they all watched the gravel find its way around the rocks.

"Is the jar full now?"

"Probably not," as they became suspicious.

Next he produced a bucket of sand and poured it into the jar as well. "Is the jar full?" Hardly anyone responded.

And then the professor took a pitcher of water and emptied the contents into the jar.

"So what's the lesson?" asked the teacher.

One student said, "No matter how full your schedule you can always fit more in if you try hard."

"No, that's not it. The point is, if you don't put the big rocks in first, you'll never fit anything else in."

Figuring out the most important values we have is choosing the "Big Rocks" of your life.

When you're able to put these *big rocks* in first, you'll be able to fit in many of the "small rocks," too.

"We are paid to impact the world—not be impacted by it."

Now the Real Work Begins

By this time you should have narrowed your list of values down to 12-20 items.

You're looking to get the list down to **five**, and this requires some tough choices. It's not easy and will take some real thinking, but you can do it. Trust your intuition.

Remember, by choosing only five, you don't give up the importance of the values that don't make the final cut.

They're still your values and are part of who you are.

Hierarchy of Values

Once you decide upon your top five, you need to determine your Hierarchy of Values. Which is number one? What's number two?

You may want to play one against another. Examine one of your choices and compare it to another one. Which would you choose if you had to choose only one?

Some Helpful Questions

1. What would you absolutely be unwilling to give up?
2. What would you fight for?
3. What would you die for?
4. Would someone who knows you well see this value in you?

What you want to do is arrange your top values in order of importance.

Describing Your Core Values

Once you've ordered your top five core values, it's usually helpful and illuminating to write a brief paragraph explaining what each value means to you.

I recommend you write your descriptions in the present tense. It's more powerful. In the next chapter are examples of Value Statements others have created.

You'll want to view them in order to gain a better idea of what I'm talking about.

Michael E. Angier

Chapter 5:
Examples of Core Values

We've provided some examples of Core Values in this chapter.

A Note of Caution

Don't copy them. These samples are examples for form only. Your values are just that—*yours*.

They should reflect who *you* are. Not who you think you should be.

Note: The following are not Core Value Statements per se, but they are the stated core ideologies for visionary companies.

Direct Electronics Core Values and Beliefs

We believe the customer comes first in everything we do, and we're committed to customer satisfaction.

Our goal is to provide the customer with a quality product in a friendly, courteous and professional environment. We are dedicated to our customer's needs, and their satisfaction is our only goal.

We respect our customer's privacy and will not sell or give away personal information.

We insist on giving our best effort in everything we do. However, we see a huge difference between "good mistakes" (best effort, bad result) and "bad mistakes" (sloppiness or lack of effort).

Communication is the only prevention for poor quality and performance.

We recognize time is a precious commodity and appreciate our customer attention they have given us. We will work frugally with a sense of urgency on any matter related to our customers.

Marriott

Friendly service and excellent value (customers are guests); "make people away from home feel that they're among friends and really wanted".

People are number 1—treat them well, expect a lot, and the rest will follow.

Work hard, yet keep it fun.

Continual self-improvement.

Overcoming adversity to build character.

Hewlett-Packard

Technical contribution to fields in which we participate. We exist as a corporation to make a contribution.

Respect and opportunity for HP people, including the opportunity to share in the success of the enterprise.

Contribution and responsibility to the communities in which we operate.

Affordable quality for HP customers.

Profit and growth to make all of the other values and objectives possible.

Success Networks International

1. Our Customers are Our First Concern

We exist to serve them—to help them realize their unique potential. They are our reason to be. We are steadfastly committed to making all decisions with their welfare first and foremost in our mind.

2. Absolute Integrity and Unquestionable Ethical Standards

Our word is our bond. We build trust and we keep that trust sacred. We delight in promising a lot and enjoy delivering even more than promised. We play fair.

3. Long-term Relationships

We believe that business is all about relationship. We value and honor our relationships with customers, suppliers, employees, contractors, partners, associates and stakeholders.

4. Constant and Never-Ending Improvement

It's what SuccessNet is all about. We're dedicated to creating unequivocal excellence in everything we do and everything we produce. Our customers can always have confidence in our product and service quality.

5. Profitability and Growth

We generate profit and growth in order to make all other values and objectives possible. No profit—no purpose.

Burlington Parks Department

Responsibility — *We desire to meet the needs of the public, business clients, fellow employees and the department. We carry out our responsibilities in a manner that assures our facilities are clean, safe, accessible and attractive.*

Cooperation — *Cooperation begins with communication. We listen to those we work with and those we serve, then take the information gained to move with a sense of connection toward a common purpose. Cooperation requires appreciation, recognition, and feedback of the skills and strengths exhibited in completing the purpose. We carry out this purpose as a team.*

Adaptability — *We adjust to new or modified surroundings, policies, fiscal constraints, priorities and individuals continuing to arrive at a desirable outcome.*

Skills — *The breadth of responsibility we bear requires a tremendous amount of knowledge and skills to execute. We recognize this and foster a workplace ideology that promotes sharing of this knowledge and skills and promotes employee development and training.*

Attitude — *It's a little thing that makes a big difference. We make every effort to portray an attitude that is positive and fun, and we remind each other when our attitude needs adjusting. Attitude infects and affects everyone and everything else.*

Boeing

Being on the leading edge of aeronautics; being pioneers.

Tackling huge challenges and risks.

Product safety and quality.

Integrity and ethical business.

To "eat, breathe and sleep the world of aeronautics."

Michael E. Angier

Freedom/Independence

Personal, religious, financial and political freedom is at my core. I live a life of individuality, independence and interdependence. Patriotism.

Love

The love of—and for—my family is my bedrock. I experience true intimacy and harmony. My connection to God and my fellow man is a critical part of my growth and my joy. Family. Friendship. Relationship.

Integrity

My life is about truth and honesty. I am my word. Without integrity I can have nothing of value. I live in congruence with my core values. Without integrity I am nothing. Trust. Transparency. Openness. Personal Responsibility. Fidelity.

Knowledge/Wisdom

Discovery, growth and learning is a large part of who I am. I am on a lifelong quest for knowledge—and sharing what I learn.

Achievement

I am committed to and enjoy constant success and accomplishment.

I am always productive and contributing to my best ability. I am responsible for the results I produce and the actions that create those results.

Michael & Dawn Angier (their relationship)

Trust: *We trust completely in one another and work diligently to maintain and build that trust. We recognize that this trust is dearly won and easily lost.*

Commitment: *Our word is our bond. We take our commitment seriously and honor one another by keeping all our commitments to one another—both large and small.*

Intimacy: *We delight in and enjoy our physical and emotional intimacy and share it only with each other.*

Growth: *We consider our primary purpose to support each other in our personal and professional growth.*

Fun: *We strive to make every aspect of our lives fun—not only for each other but for those around us as well.*

Chapter 6:
Your True Purpose

I've written another book about purpose that goes much more in depth on the subject. It's called *Discover Your Empowering Purpose*. But because core values plays such a big role in discovering your purpose, I wanted to broach the subject here.

Bucky Fuller once said, *"Your true purpose will forever remain obscure."*

This statement bothered me for a number of years. You see, I wanted to know my true purpose more than *anything*.

My greatest fear was to reach the end of my life and not feel that I had accomplished it—or worse yet, not even known what it was.

Today, I'm more comfortable with what Bucky said.

I think he was saying that we're involved in a much bigger game and purpose than we could ever possibly imagine from our limited perspective.

> *"Efforts and courage are not enough without purpose and direction."*
> —John F. Kennedy

41

For example, as far as the bumblebee is concerned, its true purpose is to gather nectar. But we know that its larger purpose is to pollinate flowers.

If that's the case for the bumblebee, I suspect it's probably true for us as well.

I think our purpose is probably much larger than we can fathom—at least from this point in time.

Some things aren't to be understood until later. Our lives are lived forward but usually only understood backwards.

But that shouldn't stop us from going after what we consider to be our true mission or purpose. Because as we "harvest our nectar," we're almost assuredly accomplishing other things as well.

The French call it our "raison d'etre." It's our reason for being.

And the key is to affect our purpose and enjoy the journey as we do so.

So again, we embark on a challenging task. It's not an easy assignment and it's certainly not one that we should take lightly.

I see my own purpose as helping people to create and live their best life—to fulfill their full and unique potential.

It's why I wrote this book and created the Your Core Values course. And it's why I do what I do with Success-Net and my speaking and writing.

I've had the same purpose for over 40 years.

A purpose is not a goal. It can never be achieved. It's more of a direction.

One can never say, "I'm done."

In fact there's a test to determine if your purpose here on Earth is complete: If you're still here—alive—it isn't.

Your purpose is something that inspires you.

It should be big enough to challenge you and yet still be believable—at least to you.

It should be a game worth playing.

Remember, you don't do this in one sitting—or even a couple of days. It takes thinking. It usually requires some "percolation" time.

And it merits annual review.

"Nothing can resist a human will that will stake even its existence on the extent of its purpose."
—Benjamin Disraeli

In the early 1900s, the railroads were the dominating industry in America.

They controlled huge amounts of capital and wielded great power. To have a "railroad job" was to have the most secure job you could have.

As trucks and planes began to take business away from the railroads, the railroad tycoons looked upon them as competition.

And eventually, they watched their wealth and their influence seep way.

The problem was that they saw themselves in the *railroad business*. They believed their purpose was to build and run railroads.

Makes some sense, right?

But had they seen themselves in the *transportation* business, they would have invested in trucking companies and later airlines—maybe even ships, to perpetuate their purpose.

It would have been a natural progression of someone in the transportation business. Their business and industry would have evolved. Instead, they participated in their own demise.

We still have railroad companies, of course, but they are not the powerhouses they once were. They didn't understand their true purpose. And their near-sightedness was their undoing.

That's why it's important for you to have a purpose that can survive the changes in technology and culture that will surely occur over your lifetime.

With a big enough and clear enough purpose, the *way* you affect your purpose may change—but your true purpose likely will not.

So this is a time to think BIG.

Action Steps

- Ask yourself what your true purpose is. Remember, you are not to invent it but rather discover it.

- Charge your subconscious mind with the task of revealing your purpose to you. Ask for the revelation before going to sleep at night.

- We find what we're looking for. Expect to get answers and you will.

And take a look at the book description in the back of this book for *Discover Your Empowering Purpose*. Grab a copy for yourself.

Michael E. Angier

Chapter 7:
Meaning—What's it All For?

This chapter is a bit more philosophical. Most of what we've been working toward throughout this book is to experience more meaning, significance and passion in our life.

The whole reason for getting clear on our values and our purpose is to live a life that has meaning—a life we experience as fun, joyful and exciting.

Life is Too Short . . .

. . . *not* to do something meaningful.

We don't just want to make a living; we want to make a LIFE—a life filled with meaning and passion.

Here's what I mean by meaning. Meaning lives within our own minds. It's individualized. What has value and meaning to one person is not the same for another.

We Assign Meaning to Everything

What makes a table a table is us saying that it's a table.

To someone who's never seen a table, it's just a construction of boards—and that's assuming they've seen boards before.

This whole idea of assigned meaning is something that creates difficulty for us as well as makes our life easier.

So it's a double-edged sword. It depends upon our perspective and our ability to discern clearly.

Perspective Matters

In "The Phantom Tollbooth," Norton Juster tells the story of a boy named Milo, who travels the Kingdom of Knowledge. Everywhere he goes, Milo learns life lessons from a bewildering set of bemusing characters.

One of the characters, Alec Bing, offers a lesson in perspective:

"From here that looks like a bucket of water," Alec said, pointing to a bucket of water, "but from an ant's point of view, it's a vast ocean, from an elephant's, just a cool drink and to a fish, of course, it's home.

So, you see, the way you see things depends a great deal on where you look at them from."

It's not that one meaning is good and another is bad; it's more a matter of it being useful or not—helpful or unhelpful.

The bottom line is you get to choose what has meaning to you and what matters to you.

What Has Meaning in Your Life?

This conversation about meaning is an opportunity to review what's important to you—to take another look at what you've chosen as your Compelling Core Values.

Since these are the values you'll be constructing your life with, you should have confidence that you've chosen wisely.

> *"Since these are the values you'll be constructing your life with, you should have confidence that you've chosen wisely."*

When we know who you are, where you're going and why you're going there, you have more of a sense of meaning and worth.

> *"When we know who you are, where you're going and why you're going there, you have more of a sense of meaning and worth."*

You're more conscious of what goes on and what it means to you and your mission.

A life of meaningful experiences is a life well lived.

How sad it must be for some people to reach the end of their days and not feel a sense of fulfillment.

To wonder about what their life was for and have regrets about not having made more of a contribution must be a "hell" of the worst kind.

You Find What You Look For?

As I've said many times, you find what you're looking for.

If you know what your values are and what your purpose is, you'll find value and meaning in everything.

When things go well, you'll experience it as good. When things *don't* go as planned, you'll experience that as good, also.

Both your failures and successes will have meaning because you have direction and confidence in your success.

You are Worthy

You deserve to live a life of purpose and meaning. You deserve to experience the rich depth of a life well-lived—your BEST life.

"You deserve to live a life of purpose and meaning. You deserve to experience the rich depth of a life well-lived—your BEST life."

It All Comes Together

This is where your hierarchy of your Compelling Core Values, your clear purpose, your intentions and your commitment come into play. This is where they guide you in having meaning in your life.

Action Step

Take a few moments to revisit your top five values.

Post them somewhere where you'll see them and weigh their significance in the light of some time and reflection about who you are and what your purpose is.

It is this clarity of purpose and values that provides the foundation for real meaning in your life.

"It is this clarity of purpose
and values that provides the
foundation for real meaning in
your life."

I encourage you to journal about your experience and your observations.

Your clarity will lead you to a more powerful place. Your confidence will increase. You'll be more alert and aware. You'll walk in the comfort of knowing you matter and that you're making an important difference in the world.

As Shakespeare wrote in *As You Like It*: "Sweet are the uses of adversity, Which like the toad, ugly and venomous, Wears yet a precious jewel in his head; And this our life, exempt from public haunt, Finds tongues in trees, books in the running brooks, Sermons in stones, and good in everything."

> *"Sweet are the uses of adversity, Which like the toad, ugly and venomous, Wears yet a precious jewel in his head; And this our life, exempt from public haunt, Finds tongues in trees, books in the running brooks, Sermons in stones, and good in everything."*
>
> —Shakespeare

Chapter 8:
Find Your Passion

---

*"Catch on fire with enthusiasm
and people will come for miles
to watch you burn."*
—John Wesley

One would be hard-pressed to come up with a more dramatic example of someone who epitomized the above John Wesley quote than Steve Irwin.

You know him even if you don't immediately recognize his name. His show was seen in more countries than any other nature show in the world. He might have been a little over the top for some people, but there was no doubting his passion for reptiles.

I once watched a Larry King Live interview with Steve Irwin where Larry said to him, "You really like crocodiles, don't you?" Steve practically jumped out of his seat and shouted, "No no, I LOOOOOOVE crocodiles!"

Surely he had a great deal of knowledge, but his claim to fame—what set him apart from all the other experts—was his *unbounded* enthusiasm for what he did.

Who do you know who is passionate about their life? Even if you don't share their particular brand of passion, they're fun to be around, aren't they?

I'm not talking about people who just *act* enthusiastically. I'm talking about people who have a genuine passion and zest for life.

Years ago someone told me that enthusiasm should be 90% inside and only 10% outside. That way it's always bubbling to the surface and it never appears put-on or faked.

It's a sad fact that people who truly live their life fired with excitement and passion are in such a great minority. Unfortunately, most people go through life purposeless, passionless and devoid of enthusiasm—at least for the things that are important.

I find it mind-boggling that so many people get more excited about sporting events than their own lives.

These people can talk for hours, in excited tones, about someone else's game, yet they can't seem to get excited about their *own* game—**their life.**

The word enthusiasm is derived from the Greek word en-theos which means "God within". And that's what I like to think enthusiasm is—God, your Truth and your soul, coming forth.

It's Contagious
Is yours worth catching?

Would your friends describe you as an enthusiastic person? Do you feel passionate about things? What are those things?

Life should be an adventure. It should be interesting and meaningful. It should be something you're excited about. So what *are* you excited about? And why?

Through these chapters, we've been laying the groundwork for living a meaningful life filled with passion.

When you're clear about who you are and what you care about, when you have a clear and meaningful purpose, when you know where you're going and why you're going there, you have positioned yourself to live an impassioned life.

But there's another piece . . .

You must *believe* in your purpose and in its value. You must have strong reasons for affecting your purpose.

You gotta believe. You have to believe that you really can achieve that which you set out to accomplish.

All too often, I see people get reacquainted with their dreams and get fired up about going for them. But it doesn't last. They get knocked down by a few setbacks, they get tired, someone tells them they'll never make it—all kinds of things nibble away at their new-found enthusiasm.

Being Excited isn't Enough

The fake-it-'til-you-make-it enthusiasm just won't last. It won't weather the storms.

"The fake-it-'til-you-make-it enthusiasm just won't last. It won't weather the storms."

Real passion—the sustaining kind—has to be built. It can't be plastered on or faked.

Those who maintain their enthusiasm, those who persevere in the face of difficulties, those who succeed, are the ones who have positioned themselves to succeed.

You Need All of it!

No one can be talked out of their dream if they have the desire, the character, the clarity, the commitment and the passion to win.

If you're not excited about your purpose and your goals in pursuit of that purpose, you may not have found your true calling.

Or maybe you've found your true purpose, but you lack some of the other pieces to stoke and fuel your fires. If that's the case, you may need to go back and see what you've missed.

You Deserve to Win

You are worthy of an impassioned life. You are meant to operate at your highest and best and to have fun doing so.

Accept nothing less!

It's time to do the things that make your heart sing. When you do, everything becomes easier. Work feels more like play. Problems become challenges. Your life just plain works.

I've always loved an affirmation written by Charles Fillmore, one of the founders of Unity School:

"I fairly sizzle with zeal and enthusiasm. I spring forth with a mighty zest to do the work that must be done by me."

And he wrote this affirmation *in his eighties.*

"I fairly sizzle with zeal and enthusiasm. I spring forth with a mighty zest to do the work that must be done by me."
—Charles Fillmore

You Have to Take Care of Your Environment

Get around—and stay around—positive people. Don't give in to pity parties. Stay focused on what you want and why you want it.

Look at each setback as a learning experience.

Ask yourself: "What worked, what didn't, what's next?"

Build your belief by reading about others who have done great things. Listen to music that inspires you. Study your trade. Devote yourself to becoming an expert in your chosen field.

The Passion Zone

In doing these things, you'll spend more and more of your life in the "passion zone." Your enthusiasm will attract people who can help you achieve your goals. You'll be an inspiration to them and to others.

You'll have more fun and accomplish more.

Action Steps

1. Make a list of at least three things you feel passionate about. Things you have enthusiasm for and get excited about just thinking and talking about them.

2. After each one, write down why you feel so impassioned about them. What's the *value* they have in your life?

This exercise will give you insight into the things that turn you on and will help you in selecting goals that you're excited about.

Chapter 9:
Graduation

Are you ready to walk down the aisle? Can you hear "Pomp and Circumstance" playing in the background?

You're about to graduate from this course. We've covered a lot of ground.

As you've seen, the process of getting clear on, narrowing down, articulating and then living your core values is not really very complicated.

It's also not easy.

If you've done the work, you know this to be true. If you haven't, I urge you to go back and take those steps you skipped.

By now you should have started to see some results from your hard work. You have more clarity as to how you present yourself and/or your company. Your message is sharper and more effective. Your decisions are easier to make because you know what's important and what matters most.

You also have a better sense of what you need to do and the way you want to do it. You're more valuable in the marketplace because your values, your purpose and your mission are clear. Your confidence is higher.

But the job's not done . . .

CANI

It's an ongoing—and never-ending process. CANI stands for Constant And Never-ending Improvement

Your core values and your purpose need refinement over the years. They warrant revisiting from time to time to check yourself and measure what you're doing and what's important to you against your stated values and purpose.

Socrates supposedly said, "The unexamined life is not worth living."

One could also say the *unlived* life isn't worth examining.

I suspect the best is a balance.

Live and reflect, reflect and live.

If things are difficult, go back to this work and see where there may be incongruence between what you're doing and the choices you made in this process.

Visible is Memorable

Your hard work won't be as effective if you don't keep your five core values and your purpose statement in front of you.

Post them over your desk, on the visor of your car, in the front of your journal—anywhere where you will see them often. I like to move them around a bit so they don't become invisible by their familiarity.

I hope we've been able to accomplish this together.

And if your Compelling Core Values are not yet clear to you, then that's your mission for now.

Congratulations on completing this process. I wish for you to know and live your Compelling Core Values, your Empowering Purpose, have a Meaningful Mission, live your Vivid Vision, accomplish great things and feel the happiness, fulfillment and satisfaction that comes from a life well lived.

You can do it! You deserve it!

Have fun!

Action Step

Set a reminder in your calendar for six months from now to revisit the information we've presented.

Thoughtfully look over your five core values, the statements that describe each one and your purpose statement. Make adjustments to it if you need to or modify your actions based upon what you've created.

Do this for yourself, and if you own or manage a company, do it for your business as well. It pays big dividends.

A Very Useful Tool

I created a template for Microsoft OneNote as a way to keep all my personal development, ideas, goals, core values, purpose, mission and vision statements, etc., all in one place—and much more.

It's called The Best Life Navigator™ and it really pulls everything together quite nicely. It's like a dashboard for living your best life. The Best Life Navigator will keep you *much* more organized, focused and directed. It's a powerful tool.

And as a reader of this book, you get 50% off the current price when you use the coupon code COREVALUES. It comes with three valuable bonuses that I'm sure you will find useful. You can find out all about The Best Life Navigator at . . .

www.BestLifeNavigator.com

The main thing to keep in mind is to have your Compelling Core Values be a constant and uplifting reminder of the life you are choosing to live—and the reason for doing so.

A Thank You and a Request

Thank you for reading my book! I really appreciate your feedback, and I love hearing what you have to say.

I need your input to make the next version of this book—and my future books—better.

Please leave a brief and helpful review on Amazon to let me know what you thought of the book. Only about one in a thousand readers leave a review. I hope you will be a one-in-a-thousand reader.

You can use this link:
www.SuccessNet.org/go/amz-author

Thank you very much.

Michael E. Angier

BeYourBest@SuccessNet.org
www.SuccessNet.org

About the Author

Michael E. Angier is the founder and CIO (Chief Inspiration Officer) of SuccessNet based in the Tampa Bay area of Florida. He's a father, grandfather, husband, writer, speaker, entrepreneur, coach and student.

He's the author of the *101 Best Ways series, The Achievement Code, The Secret to Being Fiercely Focused, How to Create a Vivid Vision for Your Life, Discovering Your Empowering Purpose, How to Create Your Meaningful Mission* and others.

Michael's work has been featured in numerous publications such as *USA Today, Selling Power, Personal Excellence* and *Sales & Marketing Excellence* as well as dozens of electronic publications. He's been interviewed on both TV and radio many times.

And his internationally popular articles have earned him a Paul Harris Fellowship with Rotary International.

Angier has experienced personal and professional success, but he's also suffered some bitter defeats. Although certainly preferring the former, he feels that he's learned the most from his struggles and disappointments. He feels that life's greatest lessons are learned by overcoming the obstacles in the path of a challenging and worthwhile objective.

Michael's passion is human potential. He believes fervently in the indomitable human spirit and revels in helping people and companies grow and prosper.

Over the past 40 years, Michael has devoted himself to studying what works and has been an ardent student of the principles of success. He's taught seminars and conducted workshops on goal setting, motivation and personal development in six countries.

Michael feels that there are three things essential to living a fulfilling and successful life: a purpose to live for, a self to live with and a faith to live by.

Michael is married to Dawn Angier—his partner, best friend, mentor, teacher, student and confidante. They have six adult children and five grandchildren. Michael enjoys tennis, reading, writing, publishing and helping people realize their dreams.

Mistakes Happen

We're committed to publishing inspiring, practical and professional books. However, mistakes do occur. If you should find a typographical, grammatical or factual error, we would be most grateful if you let us know. And, if you are the first to tell us about it, we'd be happy to send you a thank you gift.

Just email your find with the book name, location and type of error to BeYourBest@SuccessNet.org with "Found This!" in the subject. Thanks for your help.

Other Books by Michael Angier
www.Amazon.com/author/michaelangier

The Achievement Code
The 3C Formula for Getting What You Truly Want

A simple, but proven, formula for getting what you truly want. With the Three C's, the author has distilled down from both ancient and modern teachers the true alchemy of success and achievement.

Whether they realized it or not, every single person who has ever achieved great things has employed the Three-C Formula. But not until Angier identified the Three Cs did the formula reveal itself. *The Achievement Code* outlines in simple, straightforward steps how to practice Clarity, Concentration and Consistency and actually get what you really want. Best-selling author, says, "It contains the basic principles of success upon which Michael has built his own ultra-successful life and business and upon which anyone else can do the same. In fact, if one will follow all three of the "C's" he teaches us, I cannot see how it would be possible not to succeed."

Michael E. Angier

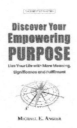

Discover Your Empowering Purpose
Live Your Life with More Passion and Commitment

Mark Twain claimed, "The two most important days in your life are the day you are born and the day you find out why."

You have an Empowering Purpose for your life. You only need to discover and uncover what it is.

This book helps you do that. You might even find it in a single weekend. And in doing so, you can live with more meaning, significance and fulfillment. You will have more confidence, exhibit more courage and have more commitment because you are fulfilling your purpose.

The author leads you by the hand as you determine your unique and special abilities and eventually your particular Zone of Genius.

Knowing and understanding your Empowering Purpose is a true game changer. If you're looking for more direction, inspiration, motivation, determination and devotion, read this book, go through the exercises and watch your life catch on fire.

The Secret to Being Fiercely Focused

How to Have More Energy, Less Stress and
Get More Done by Tackling Your Tolerations

Are You Ready to Declutter Your Mind?

The Life-Changing Magic of Tidying Up: The Japanese Art of De-cluttering and Organizing, has been off and on the New York Times Best Seller list for years—mostly on. If decluttering your home and office is life-changing, what about decluttering your *mind*?

Hundreds of thousands of books have been written on success—about what you need to get ahead. But what isn't talked about much is *what you need to get rid of*.

These niggly, spirit-sucking, energy-draining, peace-killers steal—often quite without detection—our joy, our happiness, our energy and our focus.

They are called Tolerations—things we tolerate, but shouldn't. And like weeds in a garden, we must recognize them for what they are and hoe them out—or they will take over our garden (life).

Michael E. Angier

www.Amazon.com/author/michaelangier

Do You Have a Clear Vision for Your Life?

How to Create a Vivid Vision for Your Life gives you the impetus, the tools and the guidelines to create a meaningful, inspiring and detailed vision for your best life.

The author takes you by the hand and helps you dream big, think big and act even bigger.

This book will help you to . . .

- create a clear picture of the life you wish to create
- have more clarity and direction
- make better decisions and make them more easily
- have a bigger, better life
- have more balance in your life
- always know where you're going and what you want to achieve
- have more meaning and significance
- be more inspired, focused and motivated
- have more happiness by living on your terms

Don't let another day go by without creating a Vivid Vision for Your Life. Get your copy of this book now and make the rest of your life the best of your life.

www.Amazon.com/author/michaelangier

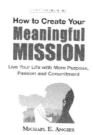

This Book is for You if You . . .

- want to maximize your time, energy and effort in a worthwhile cause—your best life!
- aren't satisfied with an average life—you want something bigger and better than that.
- want greater clarity for the path your life takes.
- desire to create a legacy—an exceptional life of meaning and significance—one that truly matters.
- are committed to creating a mission based upon your core values, strongly held beliefs and empowering purpose.
- desire to think bigger and believe in the possibilities of living up to your full and unique potential.
- want to believe more in yourself and in what's possible.
- have a desire to dig deeper, think more comprehensively and live in a more balanced, meaningful and significant fashion.

Free Resources

Personal Achievement Assessment

Download this free tool from SuccessNet. With it, you'll be able to evaluate yourself in many different areas of your life and find even more ideas for living your Empowering Purpose. Consider it your personal success inventory (PDF format).
www.SuccessNet.org/psa

Subscribe to SuccessNet.org at No Cost

If you would like to be part of SuccessNet, you can subscribe for free at www.SuccessNet.org

We offer a valuable gift like a book, special report or eCourse (it changes regularly) to anyone who joins our mailing list. And three to five times a month, you will receive an article from Michael on a topic in support of living your best life. And there are hundreds of articles, resources, recordings and more available on the website.

You can also follow SuccessNet on Facebook at www.Facebook.com/ILikeSuccessNet or Michael's personal page at www.Facebook.com/michaelangier

Acknowledgements

I am truly grateful for my wife, Dawn, who is my business and life partner as well as my best friend. She provided not only encouragement and feedback, but also her highly professional copy editing and technical expertise. She always makes me—and my work—look better.

In addition, I wish to thank the tens of thousands of subscribers and members of SuccessNet.org, who over the past 24 years, have followed me and supported our efforts in helping us all create and live our Best Lives.

You are a great source of inspiration to me. And your patronage has allowed me to do work that I love for over two decades.

Printed in Great Britain
by Amazon

58561850R00047